DIGGING UP THE PAST

The VALLEY of the KINGS

PETER A. CLAYTON

WAYLAND

DIGGING UP THE PAST
Biblical Sites • Bodies from the Past • Pompeii and Herculaneum • The Search for Dinosaurs • Troy and Knossos • The Valley of the Kings

Cover background: This is a detail from a wall-painting in the tomb of Horemheb (see page 29). It shows the pharaoh on the left, holding pots, and the goddess Isis to the right.

Cover inset: The famous golden burial mask of Tutankhamun. See more of the tomb's treasures on pages 22–7.

Title page: Detail of the back panel of Tutankhamun's throne showing him seated whilst his wife, Ankhesenamun, anoints him with perfume.

Series and book editor: Geraldine Purcell
Series and book designer: Joyce Chester
Book consultant: Dr M. L. Bierbrier, Assistant Keeper of Egyptian Antiquities, British Museum, London
Picture Research: The Author

© Copyright 1995 Wayland (Publishers) Ltd

First published in 1995 by Wayland (Publishers) Ltd, 61 Western Road, Hove, East Sussex, BN3 1JD, England

British Library Cataloguing in Publication Data

Clayton, Peter A.
Valley of the Kings. – (Digging up the Past)
I. Title II. Bull, Peter III. Series
932

ISBN 0 7502 1431 7

DTP design by: Joyce Chester
Printed and bound by L.E.G.O. S.p.A., Vicenza, Italy.

Picture acknowledgements
The publishers would like to thank the following for allowing their photographs to be reproduced in this book: Werner Forman Archive 25 (centre, right), 27 (bottom), 28, 32 (bottom); Griffith Institute, Ashmolean Museum 23 (top), 24–5, 26 (top, bottom left), 45; Robert Harding Picture Library *title page*, 27 (top); Peter Saunders 7 (bottom), 44; Topham 31 (right); Wayland Picture Library *cover inset*, 22 (J. Waterlow). All other photographs, including the *cover background*, were provided by the author. All artwork is by Peter Bull.

Contents

Belzoni – the first explorer

Giovanni Belzoni, an Italian archaeologist, was the first person to explore and excavate in the Valley of the Kings properly, between 1816 and 1819. There he made some remarkable discoveries.

The opening of the tomb

18 October 1817: Belzoni wrote; *'I may call this a fortunate day ... I caused the earth to be opened at the foot of a steep hill ... about noon the workmen reached the entrance that was eighteen feet* [almost six metres] *below the surface of the ground ... the tomb was of the first rate, but I still did not expect to find such a one as it really proved to be.'*

▲ Giovanni Belzoni (1778–1823), the first person to begin to explore the Valley of the Kings in detail and to publish his finds. He found many tombs (see pages 28 and 30).

Once the entrance was cleared, Belzoni passed through a painted corridor, went down a seven-metre stairway, on through another long painted corridor and was then stopped by a deep pit. An ancient rope and beam of wood across it *'crumbled to dust on touching them'.* The pit was there to catch rainwater flooding into the tomb, and to fool any tomb robbers.

The next day, with two beams of wood brought from a nearby village, Belzoni crossed the pit and went on down through corridor after corridor. Everywhere paintings of mysterious gods on the walls were visible by the light of the flickering torch he carried.

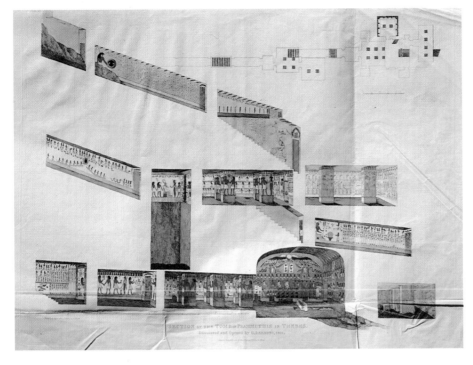

◄ Belzoni's section (diagram) of the tomb of Seti I, published in 1820, showing the descending decorated corridors leading to the painted burial hall (see page 30).

A blue faience *ushabti* figure of Seti I found by Belzoni. It is inscribed with the pharaoh's name and part of the *Book of the Dead*. ▼

Eventually, 100 metres underground, Belzoni entered a vast painted burial hall. Debris left by tomb robbers centuries before was everywhere, such as bits of furniture and funerary statuettes, called *ushabtis*, but there, in the centre, was a wonder described by Belzoni as *'a sarcophagus of the finest alabaster ... transparent when a light is placed inside it ... sculptured within and without with several hundred figures'*. These were later recognized as hieroglyphics of *The Book of Gates*, a guide to the sections of the Underworld.

Belzoni did not know it, because Egyptian hieroglyphics had not yet been deciphered (translated), but he had found the tomb of the pharaoh Seti I, father of the great Ramesses II. It is still the longest, deepest and finest royal tomb in the Valley of the Kings – the story continues on page 30.

The burial place of the pharaohs

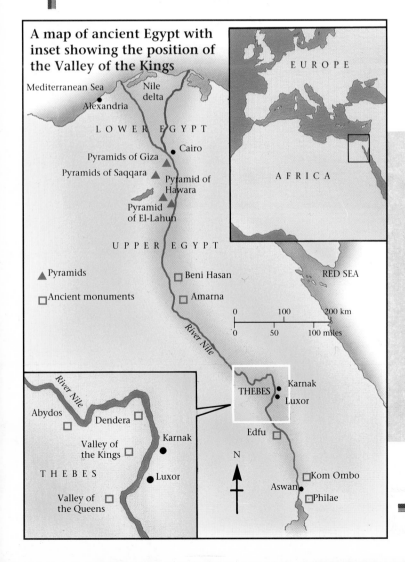

▲ The Great Pyramid of Khufu was built at Giza, near modern Cairo, about 2570 BC.

Most people think that the pharaohs, or kings, of ancient Egypt were buried in pyramids. This is only partly true. They were buried in pyramids, mainly during a period called the Old Kingdom, from about 2686 to 2181 BC. This was when all the earliest pyramids were built around the capital city of the time, Memphis. Other less well-built ones were used in the Middle Kingdom, from about 2040 to 1782 BC. Pyramids, standing high against the desert sky, were very obvious places for tomb robbers to attack.

Why was the Valley of the Kings needed?

When the New Kingdom began, about 1567 BC, at the beginning of the period known as the 18th Dynasty, it was decided to find a secret area where the pharaohs would be buried in underground tombs. A place was chosen in the south, on the west bank of the River Nile and hidden among the Theban Hills. It was in the region of ancient Thebes (modern Luxor), the religious capital. This place became known as the Valley of the Kings.

A map of ancient Egypt with inset showing the position of the Valley of the Kings

Mediterranean Sea

Nile delta

Alexandria

LOWER EGYPT

Cairo

Pyramids of Giza

Pyramids of Saqqara

Pyramid of Hawara

Pyramid of El-Lahun

UPPER EGYPT

EUROPE

AFRICA

RED SEA

▲ Pyramids

□ Ancient monuments

□ Beni Hasan

□ Amarna

0   100   200 km
0   50   100 miles

River Nile

River Nile

Abydos

Dendera □

□

Valley of the Kings □

Karnak ●

THEBES

● Luxor

Valley of the Queens □

THEBES ● ● Karnak

● Luxor

Edfu □

N

□ Kom Ombo

Aswan ●

□ Philae

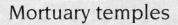

THE BURIAL PLACE OF THE PHARAOHS

Secret site in the hills

A remote valley hidden deep in the Theban Hills was chosen as the new burial site. There were only two ways in: one was a winding road, which was a dead end that led from farmland into the valley. The other way was a narrow path that came over the top of the hills, leading from the village of Deir el-Medina. This was where the workers who cut, carved and painted the royal tombs lived. Both ways were guarded by the necropolis (cemetery) guards.

▲ **The Valley of the Kings. In the centre, surrounded by a low stone wall, is the entrance to the tomb of Tutankhamun (see pages 22–7).**

The great complex of temples at Karnak, dedicated to the god Amun-Re and his family. ▼

Mortuary temples

Egyptians believed that their pharaohs became gods when they died, so temples were built to worship the pharaohs as gods. When pyramids were in use, these temples were built on their eastern-facing sides – towards the rising sun. Later, as pyramids were no longer used, the temples were built separate from the tomb, several kilometres away on the edge of the farmland and the desert. They were called mortuary temples. Each pharaoh built one for himself, but his successors often came and took away the building stone to reuse it for building their own mortuary temples in the same area. The ordinary temples to the gods were mainly built on the east bank of the Nile, where there are two temples still standing, one at Karnak, and the other in Luxor itself. Both were dedicated to the chief of the Egyptian gods, Amun-Re.

▲ The *Quorn*, or the 'Lady of the Peak', shaped as a natural pyramid, rises above the Valley of the Kings.

In the shadow of a pyramid

Earlier pharaohs had been buried in pyramids because the shape of the structure was an important aspect of sun worship in ancient Egypt. This was not forgotten when choosing the new burial site. High above the chosen hidden valley the hills rose into a natural pyramid called the *Quorn*, or 'The Lady of the Peak'. So the pharaohs were buried in the shadow of a natural pyramid instead of inside one built by humans. We now call the place the Valley of the Kings; in Arabic its name is the *Biban el-Muluk*.

Numbering the tombs

Not all the tombs in the Valley are royal tombs, since a number of nobles were granted the high honour of being buried there too. None of the tombs were ever finished, probably because the pharaohs or nobles died before they could be completed. Yet many have finely painted rooms and corridors. The tombs are numbered from 1 to 62, but some are not proper tombs – they may be just the beginnings of tombs that were abandoned. The sequence of numbers, started by the British Egyptologist, Sir John Gardner Wilkinson, in the nineteenth century, gives a rough idea of the order in which the tombs were discovered or excavated.

◄ A tomb with a low number must have been known and visited for centuries, and probably has been open since being broken into by tomb robbers. The highest number, 62, is that of the last, and probably most famous tomb discovered in the Valley, the tomb of Tutankhamun (see pages 22–7).

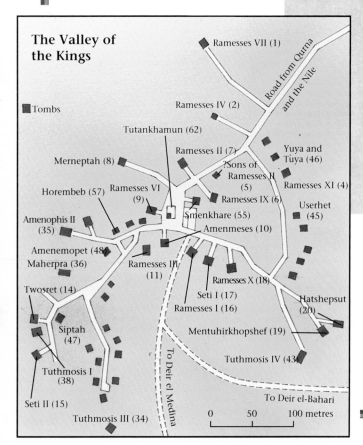

The Valley of the Kings

■ Tombs

Ramesses VII (1)
Road from Qurna and the Nile
Ramesses IV (2)
Tutankhamun (62)
Ramesses II (7)
Merneptah (8)
Yuya and Tuya (46)
?Sons of Ramesses II (5)
Ramesses XI (4)
Horembeb (57)
Ramesses VI (9)
Ramesses IX (6)
Userhet (45)
Amenophis II (35)
Smenkhare (55)
Amenmeses (10)
Amenemopet (48)
Maherpra (36)
Ramesses III (11)
Ramesses X (18)
Twosret (14)
Seti I (17)
Hatshepsut (20)
Ramesses I (16)
Siptah (47)
Mentuhirkhopshef (19)
Tuthmosis IV (43)
To Deir el Medina
Tuthmosis I (38)
To Deir el-Bahari
Seti II (15)
0   50   100 metres
Tuthmosis III (34)

Chart of royal tombs and royal mummies of the New Kingdom found in the Valley of the Kings

This chart separates the Dynasties and gives the dates of the reigns of the pharaohs and queens. You can also check the tomb numbers and when the tombs or mummies were discovered.

	Dates of reign BC	Tomb number	Modern date tomb entered AD	Mummy found AD
18th Dynasty				
Ahmose I	c.1570–1546	?	—	1881
Amenophis I	1551–1524	?		1881
Tuthmosis I	1524–1518	20 or 38	1824/1899	1881
Tuthmosis II	1518–1504	?	—	1881
Tuthmosis III	1504–1450	34	1898	1881
Queen Hatshepsut	1498–1483	20	1824	—
Amenophis II	1453–1419	35	1898	1898
Tuthmosis IV	1419–1386	43	1903	1898
Amenophis III	1386–1349	22	1799	1898
Amenophis IV (Akhenaten)	1350–1334	25(?)	1817	—
Smenkhare	1336–1334	55	1907	1907
Tutankhamun	1334–1325	62	1922	1922
Ay	1325–1321	23	1816	—
Horemheb	1321–1293	57	1908	—
19th Dynasty				
Ramesses I	c.1293–1291	16	1817	—
Seti I	1291–1278	17	1817	1881
Ramesses II	1279–1212	7	A/1913–14	1881
Merneptah	1212–1202	8	1903–4	1898
Amenmeses	1202–1199	10	1907	—
Seti II	1199–1193	15	A/1909	—
Siptah	1193–1187	47	1905	1898
Queen Twosret	1187–1185	14	A/1909	—
20th Dynasty				
Setnakht	c.1185–1182	14	A/1909	—
Ramesses III	1182–1151	11	1768	1881
Ramesses IV	1151–1145	2	A	1898
Ramesses V	1145–1141	9	1888	1898
Ramesses VI	1141–1133	9	1888	1898
Ramesses VII	1133–1126	1	A	—
Ramesses VIII	1133–1126	—	—	—
Ramesses IX	1126–1108	6	1888	1881
Ramesses X	1108–1098	18	1902	—
Ramesses XI	1098–1070	4	A/1979	—

Notes
A = at least partly open and known since ancient times.
1881 = Royal cache (forty mummies) in Deir el-Bahari tomb number 32 (9 listed here, see pages 36–9).
1898 = Royal cache (sixteen mummies) in Amenophis II's tomb number 35 (8 listed here, see pages 14–15, 39).

The first hidden tombs

The first pharaoh who we know was buried in the
Valley was Tuthmosis I (1524–1518 BC). He was the third
pharaoh of the period known as the 18th Dynasty.
Whether it was the pharaoh who had the idea of having
a hidden tomb dug in the Valley, or whether it was his
architect, Ineni, we do not know. We do know that it
was Ineni who carried out the work because he left his
autobiography inscribed on the walls of his own tomb,
among the tombs of the nobles. He also tells us that he
had two tall obelisks of red granite brought from the
quarries at Aswan to be erected in the temple at Karnak.
We know too that Ineni was especially pleased that he
had; 'inspected [supervised] *the excavation of the cliff-tomb
of His Majesty* [Tuthmosis I], *alone, no one seeing, no one
hearing.'* By that he meant the work had been done in
secret. Eventually Tuthmosis I was buried in his tomb in
the Valley of the Kings in about 1517 BC.

The tomb of Tuthmosis I was rediscovered in modern
times by the French Egyptologist Victor Loret, in March
1899. It had been robbed centuries before and only
debris remained. The pharaoh's mummy was not in the
tomb. It had already been found eighteen years before in
1881, hidden in another tomb with other royal
mummies at Deir el-Bahari (see pages 36–9).
Tuthmosis I's tomb now has the number 38.

**One of the pair of red granite obelisks erected in the temple at
Karnak by the architect Ineni for Tuthmosis I still stands there.** ▶

Not everything is clear or known about the early history of the Valley. It is thought by some that Tuthmosis I's original tomb could have been another tomb (number 20), now called the tomb of Queen Hatshepsut. She was the daughter of Tuthmosis I and wife of his successor, Tuthmosis II. It seems that the queen may have intended her tomb to be a double one for her and her father. Later a new tomb was dug for Tuthmosis I by his grandson Tuthmosis III, and the old pharaoh's body was taken there. This is the tomb found by Loret which was given number 38.

In tomb 20, cleared by the British Egyptologist Howard Carter in the spring of 1903, two yellow quartzite sarcophagi were found, one inscribed for Hatshepsut and the other for Tuthmosis I. They were virtually the only things left complete by the robbers. The rest of the finds were simply fragments and debris. Queen Hatshepsut's body has not been found and, although the mummy of her husband, Tuthmosis II, was found in 1881, we are still not sure where his tomb was.

A statue of Queen Hatshepsut as a sphinx with her name in a cartouche (the writing of a royal name within an oval shape) identifying her on her chest. ▼

The 'Napoleon' of ancient Egypt

Tomb of a mighty general

Where the first few tombs in the Valley had been dug underground, the next one, belonging to Tuthmosis III, was different – its entrance was half-way up a cliff face. A clever architect obviously hoped to defeat any would-be tomb robbers by this. Originally, there must have been a stairway cut in the rock of the cliff face to the height of the tomb entrance, so that not only the workers could come and go easily but also, when the time came, the pharaoh's coffin could be taken there.

▲ The entrance to the tomb of Tuthmosis III, high up in the cliff face of the Valley of the Kings.

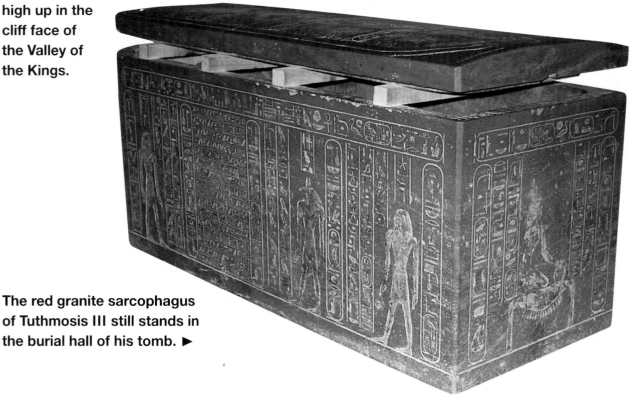

The red granite sarcophagus of Tuthmosis III still stands in the burial hall of his tomb. ▶

Tuthmosis III has been called the 'Napoleon' of ancient Egypt because of his great military conquests, like the great French general and emperor, Napoleon Bonaparte (1769–1821). Tuthmosis III led an Egyptian army all the way up through Palestine and Syria as far as the River Orontes in northern Syria, winning many battles on the way, and all within twenty-eight days. On his triumphant return, having greatly enlarged the Egyptian empire, he gave much of the booty to the temple of Amun-Re at Karnak as thanks to the god for making him victorious. A huge carved relief on the temple wall shows the pharaoh killing enemies in great numbers.

From the entrance, passageways and stairways led down into the rock to an oval, painted burial chamber where the pharaoh's sarcophagus still lies. Once the burial had been made and the doorway blocked up, the stonemasons had cut away the stone of the entrance stairway leaving just a sheer cliff face. Despite all these precautions, robbers still managed to get into the tomb. They prised off the lid of the pharaoh's red granite sarcophagus and, having smashed everything within sight in the burial chamber and the four small storerooms leading off it, took away anything that had any value.

▲ A huge wall relief on the temple of Amun-Re at Karnak shows the victorious pharaoh Tuthmosis III smiting a group of captives he holds by their hair.

The tomb of Tuthmosis III (1504–1450 BC) was discovered by Loret in February 1898 (it is now tomb number 34), but the pharaoh's mummy was already safe in the Cairo Museum. It had been found in 1881 with many of the other royal mummies (pages 9 and 36–9).

A tomb with royal guests

Amenophis II with the god of the dead, Osiris, shown on a wall-painting in the pharaoh's tomb. The pharaoh's name is above his head (in a cartouche). ▼

The tomb of Tuthmosis III's son, Amenophis II (1453–1419 BC) was found by Victor Loret in March 1898 and was given the number 35. The entrance is at the foot of the cliff in the Valley, with steep stairways and corridors leading downwards through several undecorated rooms, until the burial chamber is reached. This chamber is an oblong shape with six pillars and there are four small rooms off it, two on each side. Around the walls of the chamber are painted scenes from the *Book of the Ami-Duat*. Six pillars standing in the room have paintings of the pharaoh with various gods and goddesses, and the ceiling is covered with gold stars against a blue sky.

Although Victor Loret found that the tomb had, as usual, been robbed, it was different from the other finds made previously in the Valley. At the end of the burial chamber, in a sunken crypt, stood the pharaoh's sarcophagus and there, lying in it, was the mummy of Amenophis II. Robbers had attacked it but priests had repaired the damage and replaced it in the sarcophagus.

◄ The red granite sarcophagus of Amenophis II in his tomb, with the goddess Nephthys carved on the end, kneeling on the hieroglyphic sign for gold.

The guests are discovered

Then, examining the four side rooms, Loret found that there were other mummies in two of them – there were a total of fifteen additional bodies in the tomb. These had been brought from their original tombs by priests in an effort to save them from being damaged further by tomb robbers, and all hidden in this one royal tomb. It was not possible to identify all the bodies since several of them did not have the dockets or inscriptions on their bandages saying who they were. However, of the group of sixteen bodies, nine pharaohs and one queen have been provisionally named, they are: Amenophis II himself, Tuthmosis IV, Amenophis III, Merneptah, Seti II, Siptah, Ramesses IV, Ramesses V, Ramesses VI and Queen Tiy (wife of Amenophis III, see page 19). The other six bodies are unnamed.

▲ The mummy of the pharaoh Merneptah, son of Ramesses II, was found in the tomb of Amenophis II along with fifteen other royal bodies.

The royal relatives

▲ The gold-covered wooden inner coffin of Tuya, the great-grandmother of Tutankhamun.

Not all the tombs dug in the Valley of the Kings belonged to pharaohs or queens. There were some exceptions, for instance when a tomb might be granted as a high honour to a relative, noble or someone who had done great service.

In February 1905, one such burial was found by James Quibell working for the American amateur Egyptologist, Theodore M. Davis. Outside the main central area of the Valley are several smaller valleys, called *wadis*. It was in one of these that a small sealed doorway was found. It lay beneath piles of loose limestone chippings from later tombs dug near by. A steep passageway beyond it led down to a small chamber which, Quibell saw immediately, had been disturbed. But, it was still full of objects and there was evidence that some effort had been made to tidy up the mess after the robbery. The robbery must have been committed shortly after the burial took place. (This tomb was given number 46.)

The robbers had opened the two great shrines which stood on huge wooden sledges. They had pushed the lids of the coffins to one side in order to get at the mummies and steal their jewellery. The mummies were of an elderly man called Yuya, and his wife Tuya, the parents of the great Queen Tiy, wife of Amenophis III. No wonder they had been granted the honour of a tomb in the royal valley! Although robbed, it was the richest tomb found in the Valley until Tutankhamun's in 1922.

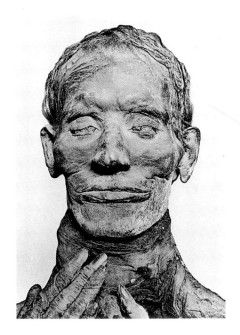
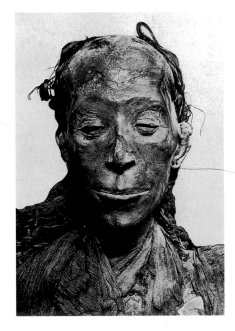

◄ The finely preserved heads of the mummies of Yuya (left) and Tuya, the parents of the great Queen Tiy, wife of Amenophis III.

All around them were all the treasured items the couple wanted to take with them to the Afterlife. Yuya, who had been an important military man, even had his chariot with him. One of the finest objects in the tomb was a small wooden chair with a scene carved on its back panel showing a princess. It gave her name as Sitamun, daughter of Amenophis III. She had used the chair as a child and then given it to Yuya and Tuya, who were her grandparents, for their tomb.

The small wooden chair belonging to Princess Sitamun which she gave to the burial of her grandparents, Yuya and Tuya. ►

A pharaoh, a queen and a mystery

A magnificent statue of Amenophis III found in the Luxor temple, among a cache of statues in 1989. ▼

Although most of the royal dead of the 18th to 20th Dynasties, known as the New Kingdom, were buried fairly close to each other in what we now call the Valley of the Kings, a little distance away is another valley where tombs were also dug. The main Valley of the Kings is actually the eastern valley, the other valley is the western valley. It was in the western Valley of the Kings, about 1349 BC, that the greatest pharaoh of the 18th Dynasty, Amenophis III, was buried in a tomb (which was given the modern number 22).

The tomb was rediscovered in 1799 by French officers in the army of Napoleon, which had recently invaded Egypt. As usual, very little remained except fragments of smashed furniture, stone debris and *ushabti* figures, all of which would have been of no interest to the robbers. The pharaoh's red granite sarcophagus had been smashed and its lid still lies in the tomb.

In 1915, Howard Carter cleared the tomb and its entrance again and, more recently in 1989–90, a team of Japanese Egyptologists did further work there.

The plan of the tomb is quite complex. It has two right-angled turns in the long entrance passageways before the burial hall, with its several side rooms, is reached. The walls are covered in religious texts from the *Book of the Ami-Duat*, which are very damaged. The tomb is not open to visitors.

The pharaoh

Although Amenophis III had not been buried in the main royal Valley of the Kings (the eastern valley), curiously, his mummy was found there in 1898. It was with the group of other royal mummies that were found in the tomb of Amenophis II, number 35 (see pages 15 and 39).

The queen

Amenophis III's queen was named Tiy. Her mummy appears to have been moved and re-buried in four different tombs. We know that her husband died before her, and she went to live with her son, the new pharaoh. He had changed his name to Akhenaten, and had a new capital in middle Egypt, at a site called el-Amarna. It is believed that Queen Tiy died and was buried at el-Amarna first of all, then her body was brought to Thebes and possibly buried for a while in a small tomb in the eastern Valley of the Kings. This tomb, number 55, was found by the British Egyptologist, Edward Ayrton, in January 1907.

Wall relief of Queen Tiy from the tomb of the noble Userhet, one of her courtiers, at Thebes. ▼

The mystery

When tomb 55 was entered, it was in a terrible mess because rainwater had managed to seep into it over the centuries. The tomb was quite small and its walls were only roughly finished. In the burial chamber was a badly damaged coffin with a decayed mummy inside it. But there was something odd about it all. The name of the dead person, which normally appears in the royal cartouche down the front of the coffin, had been hacked out. Also, the gold-leaf covering the wooden mummy mask had been ripped away. Someone had wanted to destroy the name and image of the person in the coffin.

◄ The golden face of the decorated coffin found in tomb 55 had been ripped off and the owner's name hacked out to make it unidentifiable.

It is a mystery that has still not been fully solved. Egyptologists still argue about the identity of the person left lying in the coffin, since it is now thought that there were three burials in the tomb. One burial was that of the great Queen Tiy – this is known because some of her funerary equipment was in the tomb. Her body was removed from this second place of her burial to the tomb of her husband, Amenophis III, in the next valley.

From there her body was moved for a third time to another tomb. The mummy of an elderly lady found in the tomb of Amenophis II (number 35) is now thought to be that of Queen Tiy.

The mummy left lying in the coffin in tomb 55 is thought to be of a pharaoh called Smenkhare, who reigned together with Akhenaten for a short while before Akhenaten died. The third body that was originally there in the tomb may have been Akhenaten himself, and it was taken away and hidden in another, as yet undiscovered tomb.

The beautiful head of a lady, possibly Queen Kiya, on one of the four canopic jars found in tomb 55. ▼

The mystery did not end there. The damaged coffin in tomb 55 had originally been made for a woman and not a man. It was possible to tell this from the way the hieroglyphic texts were written with feminine endings to some of the words. But who was she? In a niche in the chamber wall were four alabaster canopic jars, which were used to contain the dead person's internal organs, such as the lungs, which had been removed when the mummy was being prepared. The inscriptions on them had been removed, but the stoppers of the jars were carved with the head of a beautiful woman. We now think that she may have been Queen Kiya, a wife of Akhenaten and the mother of the pharaoh Tutankhamun. We cannot be certain of this, but it shows how research and records kept on objects that have been found are constantly changing aspects of the study of ancient Egypt.

Tutankhamun – the 'golden pharaoh'

▲ The solid gold portrait death mask of Tutankhamun, weighing 10.23 kilogrammes, that covered the head of the pharaoh's mummy.

The best-known name of all the pharaohs buried in the Valley of the Kings is that of Tutankhamun, who died in about 1325 BC. His tomb was the only one found in the Valley that was almost intact.

Howard Carter was convinced that there was at least one more hidden tomb in the Valley. He had excavated for his patron, Lord Carnarvon, for many years, at first amongst the tombs of the nobles. Then, in 1914, they received permission to excavate in the Valley itself.

Carter found very little in the first years, and Carnarvon wanted to stop; the work was costing too much money and nothing of interest was being found. Carter persuaded him to pay for just one more season, starting in October 1922, and Lord Carnarvon agreed.

There was just one small area left in the Valley that had not been examined. It was near the entrance to the large tomb of Ramesses VI (number 9), who had died in about 1133 BC. Carter and his team had not been allowed to work there because it would have interfered with tourists visiting the tomb. However, as work started early that season they got permission to clear the debris away. First, there were the usual rock fragments. Then, deeper down, they found the remains of the huts belonging to the workers who had dug the nearby royal tomb.

'Hardly had I arrived on the work next morning [4 November 1922] than the unusual silence, due to the stoppage of the work, made me realize that something out of the ordinary had happened, and I was greeted by the announcement that a step cut in the rock had been discovered underneath the very first hut to be attacked. This seemed too good to be true, but a short amount of extra clearing revealed the fact that we were actually in the entrance of a steep cut in the rock, some thirteen feet [four metres] below the entrance to the tomb of Ramesses VI ... The manner of cutting was that of a sunken stairway entrance so common in the Valley, and I almost dared to hope that we had found our tomb at last.'
Source: H. Carter and A. C. Mace, *The Tomb of Tut. Ankh. Amen*, vol. 1, p. 87.

Howard Carter (left) and Arthur Mace taking down the sealed doorway that led into Tutankhamun's burial chamber. In the darkness beyond are the great gold-covered wooden shrines that surrounded the pharaoh's sarcophagus and three coffins. ▲

The first glimpse of the tomb

A plan of the tomb of Tutankhamun. ▼

By sunset the next day Carter had uncovered the top of a blocked and sealed doorway, but the only seals on it were those of the necropolis guards. There was no royal name there. Through a small peephole made in the top of the doorway Carter could see a rubble-filled passageway beyond. Just below the cleared area there was a seal with a pharaoh's name (but Carter did not know this at the time).

With great self-control Carter had the diggings filled back in again whilst he sent a telegram to Lord Carnarvon in England. Carter took a great gamble, without knowing what he had found. The find could easily have been yet another robbed and empty tomb.

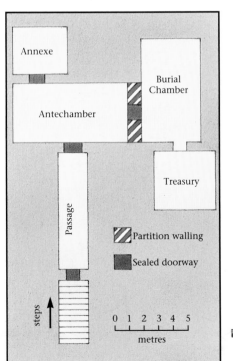

But, the telegram read:

'At last have made wonderful discovery in Valley: a magnificent tomb with seals intact; re-covered same for your arrival; congratulations.'

Lord Carnarvon and his daughter, Lady Evelyn Herbert, arrived at Luxor on 23 November, and the entrance to the tomb and its sixteen steps were re-excavated. This was when they first saw the seals with the name of the young pharaoh Tutankhamun on the lower part of the door. They could also now see that the doorway had been opened and resealed twice in the past – it had been entered by robbers. Was it empty? They did not know what to expect.

Beyond the first door, a blocked corridor had to be cleared to reach another sealed and plastered doorway. Here Carter made a small hole in the top left corner of the door and inserted an iron testing-rod, but there was only empty space beyond. Now Carter could insert a candle and peer through.

▲ The robbers' hole, beneath one of the three gold-covered couches, that led into the Annexe.

"Wonderful things"

Carter recounted his first view into the chamber:

'At first I could see nothing, the hot air escaping from the chamber causing the candle flame to flicker, but presently, as my eyes grew accustomed to the light, details of the room within emerged slowly from the mist, strange animals, statues, and gold – everywhere the glint of gold ... I was struck dumb with amazement, and when Lord Carnarvon, unable to stand the suspense any longer, inquired anxiously, "Can you see anything?", it was all I could do to get out the words, "Yes, wonderful things".'
Source: op. cit. pp. 95–6.

▲ A pendant from the tomb of Tutankhamun in the form of a 'Wedjat eye', which was the symbol of protection and good health.

A heavy gold collar and pectoral with blue scarabs and winged royal *uraei* (cobras). ▶

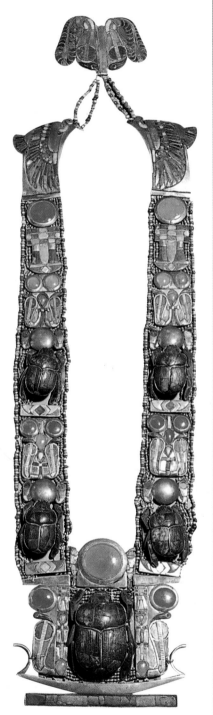

The Antechamber

When more of the second doorway had been removed the excavators saw that the room was full of furniture and statues – but they realized that there was no coffin. This was called the Antechamber and, to the right, at the end of the chamber stood two large, black wooden statues of a pharaoh on either side of another blocked doorway. Carter believed there had to be a burial chamber, or more, beyond it.

A hole in the wall beneath a couch on the far side of the Antechamber led into another storeroom, the Annexe, where the robbers had also been. First, the Antechamber and its contents had to be recorded and cleared carefully before Carter could tackle the sealed doorway between the statues.

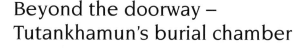

▲ Howard Carter (kneeling) opening the doors of the innermost, fourth golden shrine to reveal Tutankhamun's sarcophagus within.

A gilded statuette of the goddess Isis, who stood guarding Tutankhamun's canopic shrine in the Treasury. ▶

Carter examining the inner coffin. ▼

Beyond the doorway – Tutankhamun's burial chamber

When the first portion of the door was taken away at the top there appeared to be a gold wall just beyond it. This was the first of four great, gilded (gold-covered) wooden shrines, each enclosed within the other. Inside the fourth shrine lay the pharaoh's sarcophagus with three coffins lying within it. The innermost coffin was made of solid gold and it held Tutankhamun's mummy with a gold death mask over its head.

Beyond the burial chamber an open doorway, guarded by the figure of the jackal-god Anubis, led to the Treasury where the pharaoh's canopic chest stood. It was another room packed with objects that the robbers had rifled through.

Fortunately, on both occasions when the tomb had been broken into, they had not attacked the great golden shrines and the pharaoh's mummy. The robbers must have been caught before they could rob the mummy and were probably executed.

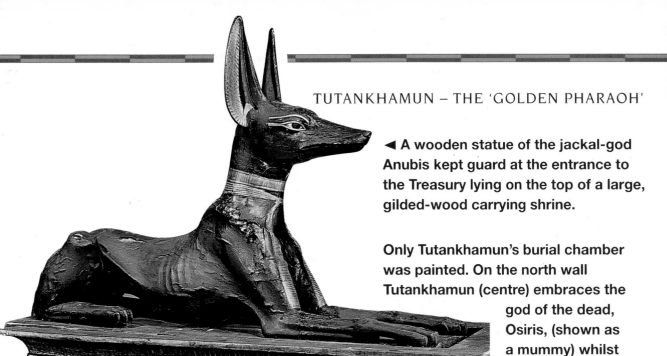

◄ A wooden statue of the jackal-god Anubis kept guard at the entrance to the Treasury lying on the top of a large, gilded-wood carrying shrine.

Only Tutankhamun's burial chamber was painted. On the north wall Tutankhamun (centre) embraces the god of the dead, Osiris, (shown as a mummy) whilst the pharaoh's *ka*, or spirit, stands behind him. ▼

Great treasures

The wealth of valuable objects packed into Tutankhamun's tiny tomb was incredible, especially because he was a young pharaoh, hardly known in modern times at all before the discovery of his tomb. We may wonder what great riches tomb robbers must have stolen from the tombs that belonged to the great pharaohs, such as Amenophis III, Seti I and Ramesses II. We shall never know.

The vizier and the general who became pharaohs

▲ **Detail from the north wall of Tutankamun's burial chamber showing Ay (right), Tutankhamun's successor, performing the ceremonies at the pharaoh's funeral.**

Honour for the vizier

The large tomb of Ay (number 23), who was Tutankhamun's elderly successor, is in the western Valley of the Kings, but the tomb was not originally intended for him. Tutankhamun should have been buried in it, but it was not finished when the young pharaoh died suddenly. Since Ay had been Tutankamun's vizier (a high official, second only to the pharaoh) he had been granted a small tomb in the Valley of the Kings as an honour. It was in this tomb that Tutankhamun was buried whilst Ay was later buried in the tomb intended for the young pharaoh.

Giovanni Belzoni found Ay's tomb in 1816, its walls and sarcophagus smashed to pieces so that little remained. However, we have a painting of Ay in Tutankhamun's tomb where, on the north wall of the burial chamber, he is shown as the new pharaoh officiating at the funeral of Tutankhamun.

The general who became pharaoh

Horemheb, who succeeded Ay, had been a successful general under Akhenaten and Tutankhamun. He had built his tomb at Saqqara, south of Cairo, which has been recently rediscovered by Professor Geoffrey Martin.

When Horemheb became pharaoh he abandoned his Saqqara tomb in favour of a larger, painted tomb in the Valley of the Kings. It is tomb number 57 and was found in 1908 by Edward Ayrton. Some of the rooms are beautifully painted and finished. Others, such as the burial chamber, are only partly painted and still have the rough outlines of the intended paintings on the walls.

Inside the burial chamber there was a splendid red granite sarcophagus, which was empty. All around it there was broken furniture and wooden statuettes. Some complete examples of this type of statue were found fourteen years later in Tutankhamun's tomb.

▲ A wall-painting in the tomb of Horemheb with the pharaoh standing between the goddess Hathor and the falcon-headed god Horus, son of Osiris and Isis.

The red granite sarcophagus of Horemheb, still in his tomb, has protecting goddesses carved at each corner. ▶

The warrior father and son

The head of Seti I's mummy that was found in the cache of royal mummies in 1881 (see pages 36–9). The great painted burial hall of Seti I's tomb is over 100 metres underground. ▼

Seti I's father, Ramesses I, had only reigned for about four years and was buried in a small tomb in the Valley of the Kings. Seti had his tomb dug near his father's, but much larger and deeper. In October 1817 it was found by Giovanni Belzoni (see pages 4–5), who had also found the tomb of Ramesses I (number 16).

Amongst the debris and broken remains of the once fine funerary furniture there were two large wooden statues of the pharaoh. Since similar ones were found in Tutankhamun's tomb, we now know that Seti's statues must have stood guard over his sarcophagus and parts of them, such as the kilt and headdress, were overlaid in gold. The robbers had stripped all this away.

The tomb of Seti's son, the great warrior pharaoh Ramesses II, is hardly known at all. It was cut into a part of the Valley where the rock later collapsed and it has not been possible to clear or explore the whole tomb. Ramesses II was certainly buried in it, but only a few fragments of the original burial equipment survive. When Harry Burton, an American Egyptologist, managed to get into the tomb in 1913–14, he recorded that he had to crawl for sixty metres on his hands and knees to reach the first chamber, but could get no further. The pharaoh's mummy had been removed to safety long before, first to his father's tomb and then to the great royal cache of mummies where it was rediscovered in 1881 (see pages 36–9).

▲ The mummy of Ramesses II was found in 1881 in the great royal cache (see pages 36–9).

New secrets from old known tombs

In 1995, an American expedition working in the Valley reached deep into a tomb, which was first found in 1820.

Howard Carter, in 1913 and 1920, had tried unsuccessfully to clear the debris blocking the way into the tomb's first three rooms.

The new excavations have revealed that there are at least sixty, possibly 100, rooms there. Carvings on the tomb walls show Ramesses II and several of his sons, he had over fifty of them. It is possible that those of the pharaoh's sons who died before him were buried in this tomb, which is only about 120 metres away from Ramesses II's own tomb (number 7). Work is still in progress clearing the passages and rooms of the debris left by ancient robbers.

The pharaoh who fought the 'Sea Peoples'

Ramesses III had a turbulent reign. It was a time when peoples from around the Mediterranean were trying to fight their way into Egypt to win land on which to settle. The Egyptians called them the 'Sea Peoples'. Great battles were fought on land and sea and the accounts of these are inscribed on the walls of Ramesses III's mortuary temple at Medinet Habu. Here there are vivid scenes of Egyptian soldiers and sailors beating the various nations of 'Sea Peoples'.

A plot against the pharaoh

On the first floor of the entrance gateway at Medinet Habu, Ramesses III had some rooms set aside for part of his harem. We know more about his harem from a report given on a papyrus called the *Harem* or *Judicial Papyrus*, now in Turin, Italy. The papyrus reports the trial of members of Ramesses' harem and palace staff when a plot against the pharaoh's life was discovered. Ramesses III actually died before the end of the trial, but we do not know whether he was murdered or died a natural death.

▲ **The mummy of Ramesses III was found in 1881 and, although it is one of the best preserved of the royal mummies, it is not possible to tell from it how the pharaoh died.**

Ramesses III grabs one of the 'Sea Peoples' by the hair as he spears him to death. ▶

◄ The great entrance to the mortuary temple of Ramesses III at Medinet Habu.

Museum pieces

Ramesses III's tomb in the Valley of the Kings (number 11) is quite large and well decorated. Belzoni collected the great carved granite lid of the pharaoh's sarcophagus from the tomb and presented it, in 1822, to the Fitzwilliam Museum in Cambridge, England. The box, or body, of the sarcophagus, weighing about thirty tonnes, was removed by the British Consul Henry Salt and sold to the Louvre Museum in Paris in 1826.

▲ The great granite lid of the sarcophagus of Ramesses III has a figure of the pharaoh on it, with the goddesses Nephthys and Isis, at either side of him.

◄ The body of the granite sarcophagus of Ramesses III is covered in hieroglyphic symbols from the *Book of the Ami-Duat*.

Deep tombs and huge sarcophagi

In the later periods, known as the 19th and 20th Dynasties, (from about 1293 to 1070 BC), there was a basic change in the plans of the royal tombs dug in the Valley. A lot of the earlier tombs had been quite small or had several passages and rooms to go through to reach the burial chamber. Sometimes the burial chamber was the only decorated room in the tomb. In this later period more of the tombs were cut in an almost straight line into the rock. The early Greek travellers who visited some of the tombs that were standing open over 2,000 years ago called them syringes, or 'hollow tubes'.

A wall-painting in the deep tomb of Ramesses IV (number 2) with the pharaoh kneeling before the sun-god Re and offering the hieroglyphic symbols of Life (*ankh*) and Truth (*ma'at*) which was a feather. ▼

▲ Many sarcophagus lids were cracked open by tomb robbers. This is the head of the granite lid of the sarcophagus of Ramesses VI (now in the British Museum).

The smashed lid of the sarcophagus of Ramesses VI in his tomb (number 9). ▼

Different decorations – obscure religious texts

In these royal tombs, the detailed wall-paintings along the passageways leading to the underground burial chamber usually depict religious texts to do with the Afterlife. The wall-painting scenes of daily life in ancient Egypt all come from the painted and carved tombs of the nobles.

Secure sarchophagi?

In this late period there was also a change in the style of the sarcophagi. Where many of the earlier ones had been large, now they became enormous. The majority that survive, or that can be calculated from their broken pieces, weigh about sixty tonnes overall – forty tonnes for the box, or body, and twenty tonnes for the lid. The idea was that once the huge, heavy lid had been slid into place, sealing the pharaoh's mummy and coffin inside, it would be impossible for robbers to prise it open again.

Cracking the lid

But robbers did succeed, usually by simply lighting a big fire on the lid. The stone expanded with the heat, and the robbers then threw buckets of cold water on to it. The sudden cold against the heat caused contraction which split the stone.

The caches of royal mummies

It is only by chance that so many of the bodies of the royal dead of ancient Egypt have survived. Although a number of the pharaohs' sarcophagi are still in their tombs and several coffins or fragments of them with royal names survive in museum collections, before 1881 only a handful of royal mummies were known.

This changed when a number of antiquities with royal names on them, such as *ushabti* figures, copies of the *Book of the Dead* and stone and pottery jars, began to appear in the antiquities market in the 1870s. Sir Gaston Maspero, a French Egyptologist, who was head of the antiquities service and Director of the Cairo Museum, became very suspicious. He reasoned that the inhabitants of Gourna, the village nearest to the Valley of the Kings, had found a royal tomb which they were quietly robbing and selling the objects illegally.

A detail from the *Book of the Dead*, showing the pharaoh Herihor and his wife, Queen Nodjmet, stolen by robbers in about 1870 from the cache of royal mummies. ►

The greatest cache – 1881

◄ A group of the blue faience royal *ushabti* figures sold by antiquities dealers that gave the clue to the hiding place of the cache of royal mummies found in 1881.

Investigations were made by the authorities and all the evidence pointed to one family, the Abd el-Rassoul brothers. Eventually, one of the brothers confessed and led Maspero not, as he expected, to a site in the Valley of the Kings, but into an empty *wadi* in front of the Theban Hills. It was just to the south of the mortuary temple of Queen Hatshepsut at Deir el-Bahari. In a corner of a cleft in the rock was an eleven-metre-deep shaft. Emile Brugsch, Maspero's deputy assistant, was lowered down the shaft and crouched to enter a low tunnel. Gaston Maspero recounted the story:

'The first object that presented itself to M. Emile Brugsch's gaze when he reached the bottom of the shaft was a white and yellow coffin inscribed with the name of Nesikhonsu ... a little further on was a coffin of ... the Queen Tiuhathor Henttaui, then Seti I. Beside the coffins and scattered on the ground were wooden funerary statuettes, canopic jars, bronze ... vases ...
The entire length of the main passage was similarly obstructed and disordered: it was necessary to advance on all fours not knowing where one was putting hands and feet. The coffins and the mummies rapidly glimpsed by the light of the candle bore historic names, Amenhetep I, Tuthmosis II ... M. Brugsch thought that he must be dreaming coming upon such an assemblage so suddenly.'

The mummy of Queen Henuttaui I, who died about 1000 BC, discovered in 1881. ►

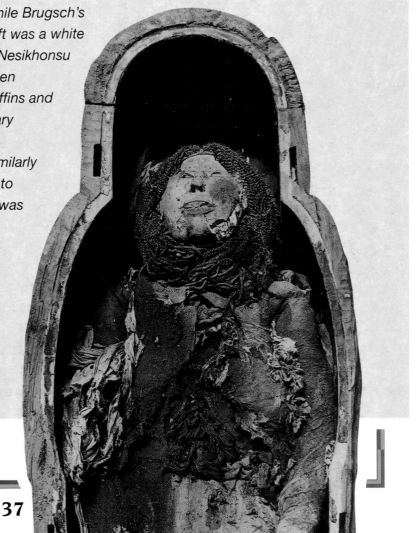

▲ The cache of royal mummies were found in 1881, hidden at the bottom of the 11-metre shaft on the left, in a valley to the south of Deir el-Bahari.

▶ The Valley of the Kings is behind the mortuary temple of Queen Hatshepsut and the high cliffs on the right. The royal mummies were found hidden in the next valley to the south, beyond the temple.

It took 300 men forty-eight hours to remove all the coffins, mummies and objects from the cache, under heavy security. Then, they all had to be carried across the Theban plain to the Nile to be loaded on to the government steamer sent from Cairo. Some of the coffins were so heavy it took twelve to sixteen men to lift them and seven or eight hours to carry them to the river, about six kilometres away.

Blue faience cups from the royal mummy cache inscribed for Queen Nesikhonsu, the wife of Pinedjem II. ▶

In fact, there was a total of forty mummies in the cache, not all of them royal. Some of the royal ones had come from the tombs in the Valley of the Kings. There were later royal mummies of the 21st Dynasty of pharaohs buried outside the Valley – but they had been moved to this tomb.

Loret's cache of mummies

The second great cache of royal mummies was found in the Valley of the Kings in 1898, by Victor Loret in the tomb of Amenophis II (number 35), described on pages 14–15. There were sixteen mummies hidden there. Again, not all of them were royal bodies.

◄ A painted *ushabti* box with large cartouches of Pinedjem I (c. 1000 BC) and some of his blue faience *ushabtis* from the royal mummy cache.

The tomb robbers

Towards the end of the 20th Dynasty, in the late twelfth century BC, there were many problems in Egypt, including riots and invasions by foreigners. There are papyri records telling of work being stopped in the Valley because of these problems. At such times it was difficult to maintain the strict security there had been in previous dynasties, and it was during that time that many of the royal tombs in the Valley were broken into and robbed. Records exist amongst the papyri of the trials of many of the tomb robbers who were caught. These records are known as the *Tomb Robbery Papyri*; more than a dozen of them have survived and over half are preserved in the British Museum in London.

Many of the robbers who were caught came from the workers' village and had found it easy to break into the tombs as they were stonemasons by profession. A number of them were caught or informed upon and brought to trial. Often they were beaten on the soles of their feet to make them confess. The papyri contain long lists of the goods, precious metals, wood, ivory, clothes and linen that had been stolen.

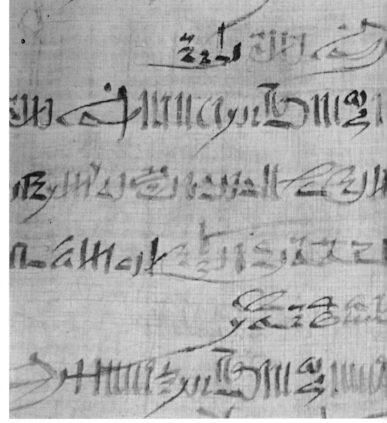

Papyri evidence

One translated account (British Museum, Papyrus 10054) records a trial:

'There was brought the quarryman Amunpnufer the son of Anhernakht, his mother being Mery of Ethiopia. He was examined by beating with the stick, his feet and hands were twisted. He said, "I went beyond the Fortress of the West of No [the fort guarding Thebes] according to my custom, four years ago. I was with … seven men. We broke open the tombs … and brought away their inner coffins which were in them. We stripped off their gold and silver which was upon them and stole it, and I divided it between myself and my confederates." '

To be caught robbing tombs carried the death penalty, and these criminals were executed by being impaled on stakes. Apparently the thought of so much buried gold was too much for some people, and to steal it they were prepared to risk being caught and executed.

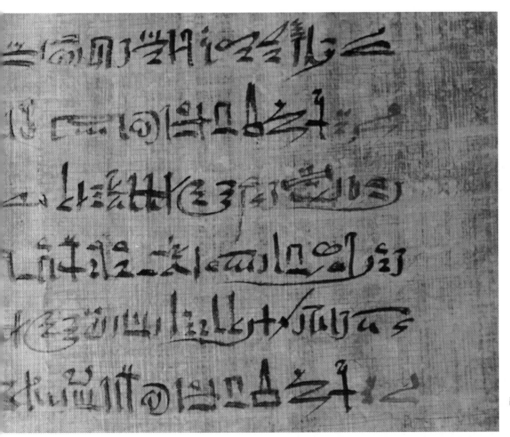

◄ **Detail from a papyrus written in hieratic, a form of hieroglyphics, recording the actual words of part of a tomb robber's confession.**

The end of the 'secret place'

At the end of the 20th Dynasty, about 1070 BC, it seems that a decision was taken to abandon the Valley of the Kings as the royal burial ground. Although the last pharaoh of the dynasty, Ramesses XI, had a tomb dug there, there is no evidence that he was buried in it.

Why abandon the Valley?

There were obvious difficulties in guarding the Valley from tomb robbers. It is also possible that, because Egypt was in a very bad state, the government itself opened some of the earlier tombs to take the valuables buried in them to help boost the economy.

The green-stone heart scarab (centre) of the pharaoh Sobekhenshaf, set in gold. It was stolen from the pharaoh's mummy by the stonemason Amunpnufer, who admitted to robbing the pharaoh's tomb and burning his mummy in c. 1124 BC. ▼

Do the great caches give a clue to the end?

The dockets and records written on the royal mummies from the two great caches show that most of the rewrapping of these mummies of earlier rulers was done in about 1000 BC by pharaohs of the 21st Dynasty named Herihor, Pinedjem and Smendes. The bodies of some of these pharaohs and their royal relatives were found in the 1881 cache of forty mummies. In several instances this cache seems to have been intended as their official burial place, that is, they had not intended to have great tombs dug for themselves elsewhere. Certainly, no individual tombs are known for these pharaohs.

The Valley – left in peace?

After being used as the royal burial ground of the pharaohs of ancient Egypt for some 500 years, the Valley of the Kings was abandoned. Once again it became a remote and silent valley in the Theban Hills, baking hot by day and freezing cold at night. That is, until archaeologists over the past 200 years, and robbers before and since then, opened the tombs. The Valley of the Kings revealed the wonders of ancient Egypt – but at what cost?

Tourists queuing outside the tomb of Tutankhamun. The tomb is so small that only twenty to twenty-five people are usually allowed in at one time. ▼

Timeline

PREDYNASTIC ABOUT 3500 BC	OLD KINGDOM 2686 – 2181 BC

PREDYNASTIC
ABOUT 3500 BC

Evidence of agricultural settlement along the River Nile.

3100 BC Menes united Upper and Lower Egypt.

Writing and metalworking developed.

EARLY DYNASTIC
BEGINS ABOUT 3000 BC

2660 BC The Step Pyramid at Saqqara built by Imhotep, the king's chancellor for Pharaoh Zoser. It was the first stone building in the world.

Trade links begun between Egypt and Asia and tropical Africa.

2589–2566 BC Pharaoh Khufu (known by the Greeks as Cheops) built the Great Pyramid. ▲

OLD KINGDOM
2686 – 2181 BC

Pepi II who ruled for 94 years, died about **2181** BC.

MIDDLE KINGDOM
2040 – 1782 BC

◄ First obelisks built.

Period of civil war in Egypt.

Karnak temple begun.

NEW KINGDOM
1570 – 1070 BC

c. **1567** BC First plans for underground tombs in the Theban Hills – the beginning of the Valley of the Kings.

1345 BC Pharaoh Akenhaten built a new capital city and tried to start a new religion.

Temple at Abu Simbel built by Ramesses II.

The 'Sea Peoples' (probably including Greeks) invaded but were driven out by Ramesses III.

Karnak and Luxor temples completed. ▼

This timeline covers important developments in ancient Egypt, and highlights some people, objects and places mentioned in this book. See the chart on page 9 for further details.

LATE PERIOD 1069 – 332 BC	MODERN AGE
663 BC Egypt conquered by the Assyrians.	**1799** Officers from Napoleon Bonaparte's French Army (which had invaded Egypt) discover the tomb of Amenophis III.
525 BC Egypt conquered by Persians.	**1816–19** Giovanni Belzoni excavates in the Valley of the Kings.
Jews in ancient Palestine establish kingdoms of Israel and Judah.	**(19th century)** Sir John Gardner Wilkinson, begins the system of numbering the tombs in the Valley.
342 BC Nectanebo, the last Egyptian pharaoh, died.	**1881** Cache of forty royal mummies found by Sir Gaston Maspero and Emile Brugsch.
GRAECO-ROMAN PERIOD 332 BC – 476 AD	**1898** Victor Loret discovers the tombs of Tuthmosis III and Amenophis II, which also had a cache of fifteen other mummies.
332 BC The Greek general, Alexander the Great, conquered Egypt.	**1899** Victor Loret discovers tomb of Tuthmosis I.
305 BC Ptolemy, the first Greek ruler of Egypt, began his reign.	**1907** Edward Ayrton discovers tomb 55.
◀ **48–30 BC** Cleopatra, the last Greek ruler of Egypt.	**1922** Carter discovers the tomb of Tutankhamun. ▶
	1989–90 Japanese Egyptologists make a further study on tomb 22, Amenophis III.
AD **30–395** Roman rule in Egypt.	**1995** US team find burial chambers in tomb 5, near that of Ramesses II. They are thought to have contained the mummies of many of his sons.
AD **476** Roman Empire collapses.	

Glossary

Afterlife The 'place' where the spirit of a dead person was believed to spend the rest of its existence.

Alabaster A fine-grained, white or almost-clear, stone which can be carved to make objects, such as statues.

Antiquities Remains or relics, such as furniture, statues or jewellery, that date back to ancient times.

Archaeologist A person who studies remains found in the earth to find out more about the past.

Architect Someone who designs buildings.

Autobiography A person's account of his or her life.

Book of the Ami-Duat A collection of sacred writings that acted as a guide for the pharaoh as to what he would find in the Afterlife.

Book of the Dead A papyrus scroll on which was written a collection of prayers or spells that would help and protect the dead person in the Afterlife.

Cache A secret hiding place.

Canopic jars Containers which held the internal organs, such as the lungs and stomach, taken from a body when it was prepared as a mummy.

Crypt An underground chamber or vault.

Debris The remains of something which has been broken or destroyed.

Dynasty A period into which ancient Egyptian history is divided. There were thirty dynasties in all from c. 3100 BC until 342 BC.

Egyptologist Someone who studies the history of ancient Egypt.

Excavate To dig something from the ground.

Faience A sand-glazed earthenware material.

Funerary To do with a funeral, or burial ceremony.

Harem The women in a pharaoh's household.

Hieroglyphics The writing of ancient Egypt which was made up of picture symbols.

Mortuary To do with the dead.

Mummies Preserved bodies which were specially prepared for burial to keep their life-like appearance.

Nobles People from the high ranks of a society.

Obelisks Tall, slim 'needles' of granite, usually erected in pairs before a temple.

Officiating Performing a duty or service.

Papyrus (plural papyri) The paper-like writing material made from the papyrus, a grass-like plant.

Patron An influential supporter of a project.

Pectoral Something worn on the chest for decoration.

Pyramids Structures with four sloping, triangular sides and a square base, which were used in ancient Egypt as the tombs of pharaohs.

Quartzite A white or grey sandstone made of quartz.

Relief A design which is raised above its background.

Sarcophagus (plural sarcophagi) A large stone box, usually with a lid, in which the coffin containing a mummy would be placed.

Scarabs The decorations or hieroglyphic symbols in the shape of a beetle.

Sphinx A legendary creature with the body of a lion and the head of a man.

Underworld The regions below the earth's surface where the Egyptians believed their dead existed in the Afterlife. The *Book of Gates* was a guide to the Underworld.

Books to read

Ancient Egypt (Eyewitness Guide series) by
    G. Hart (Dorling Kindersley, 1990)
Ancient Egypt (Family Life series) by P. Clayton
    (Wayland, 1995)
Ancient Egypt (History as Evidence series) by
    A. & R. David (Kingfisher Books, 1992)

The British Museum Book of Ancient Egypt by
    S. Quirke & J. Spencer (British Museum, 1992).
Egyptians (Young Researcher) by S. Fleming
    (Heinemann Children's Reference, 1992)
The Egyptians (Look into the Past series) by
    R. Coote (Wayland, 1993)

Museums to visit

Britain
The British Museum
Great Russell Street
London, WC1B 3DG
Tel: (0171) 636 1555
Has a royal wooden coffin and
the head of the granite
sarcophagus of Ramesses VI, as
well as many other smaller
objects from royal tombs.

Ashmolean Museum
Beaumont Street
Oxford, OX1 2PH.
Tel: (01865) 512651
Has a number of small objects,
such as *ushabtis*, from tombs.

Fitzwilliam Museum
Trumpington Street
Cambridge, CB2 1RB
Tel: (01223) 337733/332900
Has the great granite lid of the
sarcophagus of Ramesses III
and many *ushabtis* and smaller
items from royal tombs.

Egypt
The Egyptian Antiquities
    Museum
Tahir Square, Cairo
Tel: (00) (20) (2) 754319
Display of Tutankhamun's
treasures, also the royal
mummies and their coffins and
many of the objects from the
royal tombs.

The Luxor Museum
Luxor
Tel: (00) (20) (95) 380269
Has some of the objects from
Tutankhamun's tomb, and
pieces from other royal tombs.

France
The Louvre Museum
Cour Napoleon, Paris, 75001
Tel: (00) (33) (1) 40205050
Has the box of the sarcophagus
of Ramesses III, and sections
from the painted walls of the
tomb of Seti I.

USA
Metropolitan Museum of Art
1000, Fifth Avenue
New York, NY 10028-0198
Tel: (00) (1) (212) 8795500
Has a large Eygptian collection
that includes jewellery of three
minor wives of Tuthmosis III.

Smaller items from the royal
tombs in the Valley of the
Kings, mainly *ushabti* figures,
can be seen in the
archaeological museums in
Florence and the Vatican in
Italy; Berlin and Munich in
Germany, and Leiden in The
Netherlands.

Index